A-7 Corsair II

A-7 Corsair II

William G. Holder

TAB AERO

Blue Ridge Summit, PA

Aero series

39

FIRST EDITION
FIRST PRINTING

Library of Congress Cataloging-in-Publication Data

Holder, William G., 1937—
    A-7 Corsair II / by William G. Holder.
      p.   cm.
    ISBN 0-8306-3452-5
    1. Corsair II (Jet attack plane) I. Title.
UG1242.A28H65 1990
623.7'464—dc20   90-46
                CIP

TAB BOOKS offers software for sale. For information and a catalog, please contact TAB
Software Department, Blue Ridge Summit, PA 17294-0850.

Questions regarding the content of this book should be addressed to:

    Reader Inquiry Branch
    TAB BOOKS
    Blue Ridge Summit, PA 17294-0214

Acquisitions Editor: Jeff Worsinger
Technical Editor: Kathleen E. Beiswenger
Production: Katherine Brown

Front cover: Two A-7 Corsair IIs from attack squadron 46, attached to CVW-7, information
over USS Dwight D. Eisenhower. U.S. Navy photograph.

Contents

Foreword

I flew the A-7D as a leader of the famous 23rd Tactical Fighter Wing, "Flying Tigers," from 1978 to 1981. We were direct descendants of Gen. Claire Chennault's 23rd Fighter Group which flew P-40 Warhawks, with the fearsome shark teeth adorning the name, in China before and during World War II. Our A-7D's also bore the same shark teeth design, the only wing in the Air Force authorized to bear the legacy of Claire Chennault's warplanes and warriors. And we could not have had a better attack aircraft with which to carry on the traditions and legacy of the Flying Tigers.

Particularly in its early days in the Air Force, however, the A-7D did not always enjoy the reputation it earned later. In 1969 when it made its first Air Force appearance, the Air Force had its interest focused more on supersonic, air-to-air fighters and took a while to accept this Navy-designed aircraft. But the Air Force A-7D differed in two important aspects from the Navy version. The TF41 engine was more powerful than its Navy predecessor, and the automatic bombing system with its great accuracy also set it apart from its Navy version. In fact, these two features later were incorporated into the Navy's A-7E model. So, with its own imprint on the Corsair II, the Air Force could justifiably call it its own, and with this sense of ownership the Air Force fully embraced the A-7D.

It has served both the Navy and Air Force proudly. When we needed tactical airpower to go deep or fly from faraway airfields, we called on the A-7D. When we needed pinpoint accuracy to attack small, but well-defended targets, again the A-7D would get the nod. When we needed both range and accuracy to compete in the RAF's tactical bombing competition, we selected the A-7Ds from the 23rd Flying Tigers. And we won back-to-back victories in the two times we competed in 1977 and 1978 at Lossiemouth, Scotland.

The A-7 Corsair II has been an enormously successful attack aircraft for both the Navy and the Air Force for the past 20 years. As of this writing it is still in active, operational service, and upgraded versions are being considered by the Air Force for close air support missions of the 1990s and beyond.

(U.S. Air Force)

John M. Loh, Commander, Aeronautical Systems Division (1990), Lt. General, USAF

Why has the Corsair II been so successful? A number of reasons comes to mind. Its designers and advocates recognized that the required range of the aircraft, its so-called combat radius, was an important operational parameter difficult to achieve in the supersonic fighter and attack designs of the 1960s. It has been a hallmark of the A-7's success. Its designers and advocates also recognized that the accurate delivery of weapons on target could be achieved by automatic, computerized avionics, making obsolete the inaccurate, hit-and-miss manual bombing techniques of the previous 50 years. The bombing accuracy of the A-7s has been another hallmark of its success.

There are many, other, noteworthy characteristics that have made the A-7 a successful and popular military aircraft. Among them are the personality and romanticism of a single-engine, single-seat attack aircraft, for example, and its pioneering of a computerized, moving-map display in the cockpit. But clearly, range and accuracy are the two that, in this A-7 pilot's opinion, have set it apart from other fighter/attack aircraft of its day.

From its inception in the 1950s, through its introduction into fleets and air forces, to its many, many added features and upgrades over the years, the story of the Corsair II is a significant part of the story of our nation's growth in tactical airpower. It has made its name in Navy and Air Force history.

I hope you enjoy reading about the Corsair II as much as I have enjoyed flying it.

John M. Loh
Commander, Aeronautical Systems Division
U.S. Air Force

Acknowledgments

John Farquhar—Photography support

Sgt. Joe Stahl—Photography support

Glenn Holder—Editing

Public Affairs Office, Aeronautical Systems Division, WPAFB, Ohio

LTV Aircraft Products Group, Public Information Office

354th Tactical Fighter Wing, Myrtle Beach Air Force Base

U.S. Navy Office of Information

U.S. Air Force Office of Information

TSgt. Rose Reynolds and TSgt. Dave Nolan (Norton AFB)
     —Photography support

TSgt. Lori Stover, 354th TFW History Office

Introduction

Some planes are born in the strangest ways. Most of the time, a new plane evolves by picking up technology from preceding models. Such was not the case with the A-7 Corsair II. The plane was basically a derated version of its earlier brother, the F-8 Crusader. In the case of the Corsair II, "slower was better" for the new missions it was designed to accomplish. It proved on numerous occasions that it was the right plane for the tough jobs.

The Corsair II is an interesting aircraft from the development point-of-view. It was initially developed by the Navy, and several versions of the model were produced for Naval use. In fact, it saw combat service with the first model in Southeast Asia with carrier strike operations. The Navy versions of the A-7 were the A, B, and C models, but the E version would be the most used of the Corsair IIs, carrying the brunt of the attack to the enemy during the Vietnam War. The E birds would also participate in several other smaller confrontations during the 1980s. The Corsair II's time had come during the late 1980s, just as the plane was being replaced by the newer F-18.

As was the case with the earlier F-4 Phantom fighter, the Air Force would show interest in the Corsair II and would adopt a version of the aircraft for itself. There would be considerable modifications on the Air Force version, which would be coined the A-7D. This version would also see combat in Southeast Asia, but it would be confined to the ending stages of the conflict.

The plane would leave the active duty forces during the early 1980s and become the bulwark of the Air National Guard forces. In fact, new aircraft were being sent directly to Air National Guard units up until the end of production. There was even a special A-7K two-seat version built specifically for the Air National Guard. It is considered likely that the A-7 will remain at the ready with the Guard until well into the 1990s.

As is the case with most operational aircraft, thoughts of improving the plane continue. That's been the case with the A-7, but the improvement to this aircraft might evolve with improvements to the existing planes as opposed to the building of a completely new model. The proposal of the late 1980s involved a complete rework of the Air National Guard A-7 fleet with new engines, avionics and other improvements to come up with the so-called A-7F, or Strikefighter or A-7 Plus, as it has also been coined during its development. Whether or not this final version of the Corsair II will ever happen was still under consideration at the time of this printing.

This book tells the complete story of the A-7 Corsair II. Of course, it's a story that is not done. Chapter 1 covers the history of the plane and some of the decisions that were made so that it could be born. Chapter 2 addresses the technical aspects of the plane, telling the hows and whys of this very interesting and effective aircraft. Chapter 3 is the Navy chapter and covers how the Navy came up with the idea for the aircraft and evolved the many variations of the bird. The fourth chapter covers the Air Force adaption of the A-7 and discusses the changes that were made to make the A-7 also a U.S. Air Force aircraft. The use of the Corsair II in the Air National Guard service is covered in chapter 5. The use of the Corsair II in combat, with both the Navy and the Air Force, is the subject of chapter 6, while the building of the A-7F configuration is the final subject covered in chapter 7.

The contributions of the A-7 Corsair II are significant from an aircraft that was built basically by downgrading an earlier plane. But the plane has performed well and could serve into the next century before its job is finally complete.

=1=

The Beginning

CORSAIR. It's one of the most famous names in aircraft history. There has been a Corsair since the mid-1920s, including the bi-winged O2U Corsair that was active with the Navy, Coast Guard, and Marines for several years. There were more than 130 of the planes produced.

But possibly the most famous of the Corsair-named planes was the F4U Corsair of World War II fame. The famed gull-winged design won the skies in many battles over the South Pacific. The plane sported an 11-1 advantage over enemy aircraft in that titanic struggle. Production of the plane with continuing improvements lasted until 1952 with many of the planes seeing action in the Korean War. Great Britain, New Zealand, and France also used versions of that famous bird—possibly the most famous plane the Allies flew in the war. So it was fitting that the famous name should be continued into the modern jet era.

It was planes like the F4U and the A-1 Skyraider, which needed to be replaced, that initiated a study to find a light attack aircraft with a much greater range than existing aircraft as well as the capability to carry twice the payload. The study was called the VAX study, which examined the characteristics of such an aircraft. The results of the study were to develop a new aircraft with the desired characteristics, but this would take too long for the needs of the Navy. A second study conducted shortly thereafter determined that the best direction to take would be to modify an existing design for the new mission requirements.

The famous Corsair heritage is rooted in the F4U bent-wing Corsair of World War II fame and the Korean War. The Corsair II is a worthy follow-up to this great fighter aircraft.

Called the VAL study, the alternatives considered were modifications of the Douglas A-4 Skyhawk, the North American FJ-1 Fury, the Grumman A-6 Intruder, and finally, a Vought submission on modifying the F8U Crusader. Interestingly, the design would be for a subsonic aircraft, even though supersonic aircraft were in vogue during the time period.

The subsonic design was considered by many to be a giant step backward. After all, the F-105 Thunderchief of the Air Force had been designed to perform its close support mission with a supersonic-on-the-deck capability. But there was some sound reasoning for the Navy requirements. A supersonic design, it was reasoned, consumed more fuel to turn and fight at low altitudes, thus limiting its combat time appreciably and allowing for only a single pass on the target.

A subsonic attack aircraft often could outmaneuver and outlast the higher-performance aircraft design. From these considerations, the Navy argued that subsonic was actually better for this plane's proposed mission, and in the long run it won that argument. In retrospect, it's an argument that holds strong for the A-7 in the 1980s and 1990s.

Probably the most persuasive argument for the plane, however, was the fact that not requiring the supersonic capability would cut the cost of the plane dramatically. The Navy actually reported that it would be possible to acquire three subsonic birds for the cost of one supersonic version.

In the summer of 1962, then Secretary of Defense McNamara asked the Navy to work with the Air Force and report to him on the possibilities of producing an aircraft for joint service use. Later that same year, it would be determined that no research and development funds would be programmed for developing the

2

VAX design until the Navy had completed a study and proved the operational requirements for a new light aircraft.

The so-called Sea-Based Air Strike Study that evolved from the order examined some 27 different aircraft. They included vertical takeoff and landing, light attack, medium attack, and numerous other aircraft. In all, with the different ordnance and avionics combinations, some 144 programs were evaluated and priced. At the same time, Air Force and Marine Corps requirements were kept in mind as well as the possibilities for use in limited war environments.

When the first VAX designs came down, they were considered to be too expensive. Even with the existing technology that was available, it would have required five years to develop the engines and fabricate the aircraft. Those criteria led to the recommendation that the new aircraft had to be based on an existing aircraft. The aircraft was now seen as an interim, subsonic plane to be used only into the early 1970s for close interdiction and close air support of troops.

It was a tough competition, but Vought did its homework and came up with the winning design. During the proposal concept, Vought actually did a little intelligence work on its own and had a team estimate how the competing companies might end up modifying their plans for the new plane. It all fell Vought's way on 11 February 1964 when Vought was awarded the contract. It would be called the A-7 Corsair II.

The Navy looked at the A-7 specifically to replace its A-7 Skyhawk, a plane that was still considered adequate but coming up a little short on the payload capability. The Air Force watched carefully thinking that if the plane really had what it took, it could possibly be considered as a replacement for the aging F-10C Super Sabre fleet. From its experiences in Vietnam, the Air Force realized the importance of having an aircraft that could deliver the ordnance on the target as well as being able to withstand battle damage.

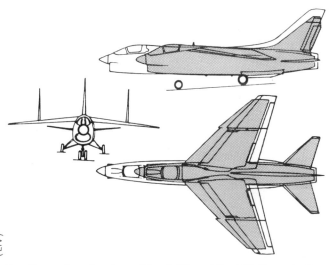

(LTV)

Comparative three-view drawing of the A-7A and the F-8 Crusader from which it was derived.

Even though the A-7 was based on the Crusader, there would be many differences. Right off the bat, it sure didn't have the sleekness of the F-8. It looked a bit on the bulbous side compared with its older brother. The changes made on the new plane were sizable. The A-7 looked shorter because it really was. Other differences from its older brother included a fixed variable-incidence wing, revised control surfaces for subsonic operations, and the installation of a completely new powerplant. The Pratt & Whitney TF30 turbofan engine would be the engine, a powerplant that had originally been designed for the F-111. With the A-7 application, however, there would be no afterburner.

The A-7 ended up having a larger wing than the F-8 with a sweepback of 35° at quarter-chord and an aspect ratio of four. It was built strong because it had to carry a massive load of external ordnance to the target.

The contract for the plane specified the importance of obtaining the plane as soon as possible. The fixed price contract carried a sliding scale of penalties for failure to meet the specifications—so much per pound of excess weight up to a $750,000 maximum, so much for excess takeoff and landing distances, and so much for every mile-per-hour under the specified contract speed. But potentially the most costly of all the constraints was the penalty for late delivery. For the time, it was $65,000 for every day late—a big price to pay.

The pressure of those contract requirements, plus the fact that a lot of time was saved by using the existing F-8 components, probably accounted in large part for the A-7's first test flight on 27 September 1965, which was only a year and a half after the contract was awarded and actually a year ahead of schedule. Vought did its job quickly and well. The A-7 was ready to go!

(U.S. Navy)

The Corsair II has had its share of combat. The A-7E Navy version saw combat in Vietnam, Grenada, Lebanon, and Libya.

(U.S. Air Force)

Outlined in the rising sun, these Corsair IIs are on their way to a strike mission in Southeast Asia.

=2=

Hows and Whys of the A-7

THE A-7 Corsair II was designed in the 1960s with state-of-the-art technology of the time. Through its lifetime, the plane has built on that firm base to keep up with the times. Here are some of the hows and whys of this great old warbird.

Wings

The A-7 has a high wing, NACA wing section 65A007, with a 5° anhedral and a −1° incidence. The wing sweepback angle is 35° at quarter-chord. The outer wing sections have a fold-up capability for carrier parking for the Navy versions and close revetment parking for the Air Force versions of the plane.

The aluminum skin is integrally stiffened by a multispar structure. The ailerons are actuated by a hydraulic system. In addition, there are large single-slotted edge flaps and a spoiler above each wing forward of the flaps. There are also integral fuel tanks inside the wings and three external weapons pylons under each side of the wing.

The A-7 wing structure is a multicell, box-type construction made of beams with heavy upper and lower skins. In the event of battle damage that could compromise structural integrity, the wing's torsion and shear forces plus the wing's bending moments would be redistributed to the remaining cells. The multiple wingtip lugs provide for flight with as many as four center-section and six outer-panel lugs missing or broken.

(LTV)

The snub-nosed profile of a number of A-7s parked on the flight deck of the USS Dwight Eisenhower (CVN-69). Clearly visible are the stowed refueling probes.

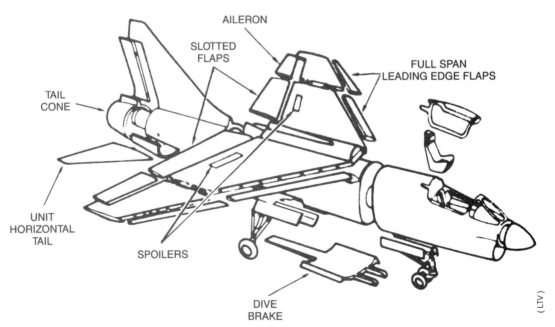

AILERON

SLOTTED
FLAPS

FULL SPAN
LEADING EDGE FLAPS

TAIL
CONE

UNIT
HORIZONTAL
TAIL

SPOILERS

DIVE
BRAKE

(LTV)

The major airframe components and subsystems of the A-7 Corsair II.

The Corsair II was originally designed with the folding wing feature for U.S. Navy carrier operations. It also proved to be an excellent attribute for U.S. Air Force operations. Note the hinge mechanism.

9

As this Corsair II rolls down the taxiway for a takeoff, the inboard slotted flaps and outboard ailerons are visible.

An arrangement of inboard spoiler-slot-deflectors and conventional outer-panel ailerons provides lateral control of the aircraft. The spoiler-deflector can also be used as a safety mechanism in case an aileron is lost. For optimum cruise and maneuvering performance, the wing has a built-in, fixed, leading-edge camber.

Fuselage

The A-7 fuselage is common to all the operational Corsair II models. It is an aluminum semimonocoque structure with the large speed brake mounted directly under the center of the structure.

The forward landing gear is a tricycle-type unit carrying two wheels and a single wheel on each of the main gears. The two main gears consist of single-wheel tripod struts. They retract forward, upward, and inward into the lower fuselage below the wing. Clamshell doors open with a mechanical interlock sequence and close by an overcenter linkage. To prevent landing the plane with the speed brake deployed, the brake was designed to retract and lock when the landing gear is dropped into position.

Self-adjusting disk-type brake assemblies, capable of handling 11 million foot-pounds of energy, slow the plane on its landing roll. A self-adjusting mechanism in each brake assembly maintains a constant brake clearance. The inner half of each main wheel contains blowout plugs to prevent fires from exploding during heavy braking conditions. Each brake system is also equipped with an anti-skid system to improve their efficiency.

The dual-wheeled nose gear is an energy-absorbing strut system that retracts rearward and upward into the fuselage front section. There are clamshell doors and a feature that locks the gear into the down position in case of loss of hydraulic pressure. The gear was designed to handle aircraft gross weights of over 32,000 pounds and sink rates of up to 10 feet per second. The tricycle gear can handle takeoff weights of up to 42,000 pounds.

The Corsair II's highly effective speed brake is located just aft of the front landing gear. The flat surface of the gear is deployed directly into the airstream by the plane's hydraulic system. Maximum deflection of the speed brake is 60° in flight, but the deflection is considerably less when the plane is sitting on mother earth.

(U.S. Air Force)

These three Air National Guard Corsair IIs are all shown with their drag brakes deployed.

The A-7's ejection system automatically jettisons the canopy before the entire seat assembly follows it away from the aircraft. The seat is stabilized in flight before the pilot is separated from the seat by nitrogen-inflated bladders.

The Corsair II fuselage bristles with electronics of all types. An ECM warning antenna is located at the end of the fairing on the vertical tail along with a similar unit at the base of the tail. In the nose section, there are the glide slope antenna, the laser illuminated target detector, and two more ECM antennae, one on either side. The forward radome carries the AN/APQ-126 radar set.

Details of the vertical tail of the A-7 show several antenna systems located in the fairing above the Ohio marking—UHF/IFF antenna and the ILS and VHF/LORAN antennae.

Certain versions of the Corsair II also carry an air starter unit. This unit could be used to start the engine with compressed air.

The aircraft was built from the beginning to sustain survivability in a combat environment. Armor protection in vital areas include self-sealing fuel tanks, optimum routing of crucial hydraulic and electrical lines, and triple-redundant, complementary back-up power control systems. The plane was also designed for minimum turnaround time with open wheelwell, single-point pressure fueling and waist-high, self-test maintenance capability that eliminates the need for complex ground support equipment.

The two-seat version of the A-7, coined the A-7K, has a 34-inch stretch of the fuselage and has a side-opening canopy covering both cockpits. The version has about an 80 percent commonality with the components of the single-seat Corsair II.

The large vertical tail is swept at 44°. In addition, there is a one-piece movable tail plane that is set at a dihedral angle of 5°. The bottom of the fuselage carries chaff dispensers mounted under the tail section. There is also an air-conditioning inlet on the underside of the nose.

On the front left of the fuselage is a retractable step mount for access into the cockpit. From its F-8 heritage, the plane is endowed with the large radome on the front of the fuselage. The main weapons are located beneath the cockpit area. Depending on the model, there are either one or two cannons. The ammunition is stored aft of the cockpit on top of the fuselage.

(U.S. Air Force, Sgt. Joe Stahl)

The large engine intake of the A-7 aircraft is very well defined from this front view. Technicians from the Ohio National Guard tend to their machine.

The adjustable capabilities of the horizontal tail and details of the A-7's slotted flaps are visible on this Air Force Corsair II. Also note the towbar attachment to the front landing gear.

You mount the A-7 only on the left side whether you like it or not. The retractable ladder gives the pilot that required tall step into the cockpit. The small divot located at three o'clock on the intake is the ECM warning system, while the dark section at six o'clock on the intake is the Glide Slope ILS System.

14

This straight-on view of the Corsair II shows the A-7's radome and forward portion of the canopy. The radome contains the AN/APG-126 Radar System.

Powerplant

There have been two basic powerplants for the different models of the A-7. The Pratt & Whitney TF30 appeared in both the P-6 and P-8 versions with thrust capabilities of 11,350 and 12,200 pounds, respectively. The P-6 version was the heavier of the two powerplants weighing in at 2,716 pounds compared with the P-8 at 2,526 pounds.

Details of the forward portion of the Corsair II. Notice how far forward the pilot sits in his director's seat.

(John Farquhar)

Later versions of the Corsair II utilize the Allison (Spey) TF41 powerplant. Again, there were two versions. The TF41-A-1 Air Force version produces 14,500 pounds and weighs in at 3,175 pounds. At 3,256 pounds, the TF41-A-2 puts out 500 pounds more thrust than the P-1 version.

The TF41 engine design features a two-spool axial-flow compressor driven by a low-pressure and high-pressure turbine. A bypass duct directs a portion of the air from the fan compressor around the combustion section and back into the exhaust. An annular mixer blends bypass air with turbine exhaust gas for more efficiency and a cooler exit nozzle, increasing greatly the threat of being attracted by a heat-seeking missile. The system has an automatic relight system that enables the system to be restarted in flight.

The maximum internal fuel for the powerplant is 1,500 gallons with 1,200 gallons carried externally. The powerplants are protected by boron carbide engine armor.

Systems

Redundancy is built into the Corsair II wherever you look. There are triple-redundant hydraulic systems and a double-redundant system for flaps, brakes, and the ever-important landing gear retraction. Engine bleed air is used by the air-conditioning unit for cockpit cooling and pressurization. The ram-air turbine produces electrical power and hydraulic pressure. The aircraft's flight control system provides control-stick steering, attitude control, and the necessary controls for accomplishing carrier landings.

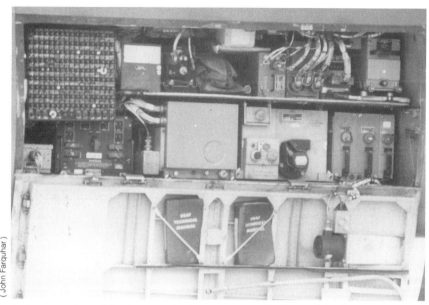

A close-up view of the lower avionics bay on an Air Force A-7D.

The lower left portion of the fuselage showing the electrical power receptacle and avionics bay.

During a chemical warfare exercise, this ground crewman inspects a 500-pound bomb underneath the wing of this Corsair II.

Weapons Capability

The flexibility of weapons that can be carried by the A-7 is amazing. It's a combination of conventional bombs, fire bombs, bomb dispensers, rocket launchers, missiles, flare dispensers, and ECM pods. In all, more than 15,000 pounds of weapons can be carried from the six wing pylons and two fuselage-mounted pylons. The outer two pylons on each wing can each carry a maximum of 3,500 pounds with 2,500 pounds the maximum capability for each inboard pylon. Five hundred pounds of ordnance can be hung on each of the fuselage pylons.

The M61A1 20-mm cannon has firing rates of 4,000 and 6,000 rounds per minute. The A-7 is one versatile machine capable of accomplishing just about any mission that it's assigned.

Performance

The maximum speed at sea level for an empty A-7 is approximately 600 knots, or about 690 miles per hour. When carrying a maximum load of bombs

18

Air National Guard technicians work on a TER on the middle left pylon of a Corsair II.

The AIM-9 Sidewinder missile has long been one of the standard missiles for both Naval and Air Force versions of the Corsair II.

and missiles, the top speed capability drops by about 40 miles per hour. The A-7 can actually carry more than one and one-half times its weight in weapons. At its maximum takeoff weight of just over 42,000 pounds, the takeoff roll is about 5,600 feet. With maximum internal fuel, the A-7 has a maximum ferry range of 2,281 miles, but that figure can be raised to 2,861 miles with both internal and external fuel. The typical weight of the aircraft is about 32,700 pounds with six MK-82 bombs and 500 rounds of 20-mm ammunition.

Avionics and Equipment

The A-7 has always been a very accurate aircraft delivering its ordnance to the target area. With the advent of the final Navy version, a great increase in that capability was realized. A fully integrated avionics package with a micro-miniaturized digital computer was added to the system. There is also a head-up display for the pilot that presents continuous solution cues for bombing and navigation on a transparent mirror directly before the pilot's eyes. This system allowed him to concentrate on his particular mission without reference to his instruments.

The aircraft's central computer system is an amazing unit that presents solutions to pilot's requests to either drop, flip, or toss bombs over the shoulder at ground targets. Also introduced in the final model was a new computer-directed

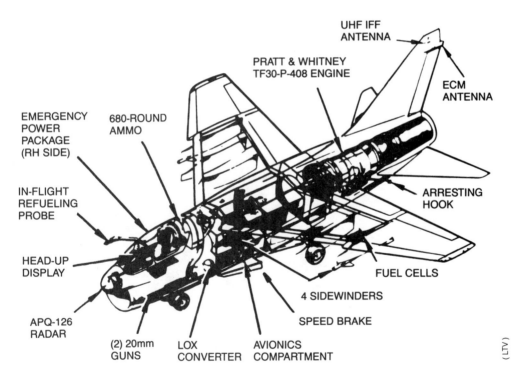

Major electrical and ordnance systems on the Corsair II.

(LTV)

20

map navigation system. The system made getting to and from the target area much more simple and more exact. The display stores maps of a selected area of the earth covering a million square miles on a single role of 35-mm film. An inertial measuring unit and a forward-looking radar were also added.

(U.S. Navy)

These two Corsair IIs from the USS Constellation are carrying a FLIR pod under each right wing.

=3=

Navy A-7s

THE A-7A was the first Corsair II of the many (1,655) that would follow. It would be used as the template for the many modifications that would be made to the plane through the development years.

The first model was powered by the Pratt & Whitney TF30-P-6 powerplant with a mission goal of providing high attack capability for close support and interdiction missions. This was accomplished by the large number of external stores locations for maximum loading and weapon flexibility.

The design range of the A-7A was about 1,180 nautical miles with an average cruising speed of 390 knots. The aircraft showed excellent flying capabilities with its high-lift system composed of leading edge flaps and single-slotted trailing edge flaps. A significant demonstration of the A-7A's capability was accomplished on 19 May 1967 when two A-7A aircraft made a transatlantic crossing to establish an official unrefueled flight by light attack jet aircraft. The distance traveled was 3,327 nautical miles in seven hours and one minute.

Some 199 A-7As were produced in addition to a trio of the prototype YA-7As. Deliveries of the A-7A began in October 1966 to training units and to the first operational unit, VA-147. The unit was declared operational in February 1967, and the aircraft was deployed to Vietnam in December of the same year.

The A-7A was also used to demonstrate the so-called *Buddy Refueling System*. The technique involved passing a fuel line from a lead aircraft back to the training A-7 and then transferring fuel.

(LTV)

The A-7A was the first version of the Corsair II. The model was powered by the Pratt & Whitney TF30-P-6 powerplant.

(LTV)

This was the first of the A-7s (Bureau Number 152580), which also was carried as one of the first three YA-7As. Note the unique vertical tail paint style. This plane would be the first of the 1545 Corsair IIs.

Three A-7As, in mothballed conditions, rest at the storage area at Davis-Monthan Air Force Base, Arizona. Many of these early models were later pulled out and modified.

Shortly after the first A-7A was delivered to the Navy, there was high-level encouragement made to the Air Force to consider also buying the Corsair II. To that end, the Air Force sent a small team from its Flight Test Center in California to evaluate the aircraft. The results of that evaluation were very positive, with the team indicating the A-7A had excellent potential as a ground support tactical fighter for the Air Force. Certain deficiencies noted on the plane were later corrected on subsequent versions of the A-7A. That, of course, would later result in the Air Force adopting the plane as well.

The B version of the Corsair II was practically identical to the A-7A with the exception of an engine substitution. A Pratt & Whitney TF30-P-8 or -408 replaced the TF30-P-6 engine. Also, variable position flaps were incorporated in the A-7B. The B version first flew in February 1968. Of the A-7B versions, 196 were delivered, the transfer being completed in May 1968. There were some initial engine problems with the A-7B, which caused a delay of their integration into the fleet to replace the A-7As.

A-7C was the designation given to the version that was initially intended to be a two-seat training version of the A-7B. The plan never took place. The A-7C designation, however, served as a stopgap assigned to those aircraft accepted with the improvements intended for the later A-7E, though they lacked the Rolls Royce TF41-A-2 engine intended for that later version. All A-7Cs carried either the P&W TF30-P-8 or -408 engines.

Sixty-six A-7C aircraft were constructed. Later, 36 of them and 24 A-7Bs would be converted into the two-seat TA-7C trainer version. It wasn't until 1975 that the first A-7C model was flown, some 10 years after the first flight of the A-7A. The planes have since been used extensively for training purposes by the Navy.

(LTV)

The F-8 Crusader roots of the A-7 are quite clear in this photo of one of the early A-7s.

(LTV)

F-7B Corsair II taking off from the runway at the LTV Aerospace Corporation for a test flight. The plane is powered by a Pratt & Whitney TF-30-P8.

26

The A-7B version substituted a different version of the TF30 powerplant, but otherwise the plane was practically identical.

The planform of this A-7B is clearly illustrated during a 1974 flight. The plane was assigned to the VA-15 Attack Squadron.

(VA-305)

A 1981 right-side, air-to-air view of an A-7B. From its serial number, it can be determined that this was the twenty-ninth A-7B produced. This particular Corsair II is from Attack Squadron 305.

(LTV)

An A-7C from VA-86 prepares for takeoff with a full load of ordnance on its inboard pylons.

The conversion to the two-seat version of the A-7 required a double stretch of the plane. Two plugs (16 and 18 inches in length) accomplished the job. It was also necessary to tilt the tail by 1.2° in order to allow the aircraft to maintain the same approach angle. A number of the TA-7Cs were also converted later from their existing TF30 powerplants to the more powerful TF41s. The first TA-7C, assigned to the Pacific Missile Test Range, was first test flown in January 1980.

EA-7L was the designation given to an additional follow-on to the TA-7C. Six aircraft (all carrying the TF41 powerplant) were converted to this configuration, which had an electronic warfare mission.

The next designation was, of course, the first version that wouldn't be carrying U.S. Navy colors. There would be many characteristics, especially in the avionics area of the A-7D Air Force configuration, that would find their way into the A-7E version.

The first 67 A-7Es had the TF30-P-8 powerplant; the first model flew in November 1968. Later E birds would carry the TF41-A-2 engines.

The A-7E carries the standard 20-mm gun and payloads of up to $7^1/2$ tons of missiles and bombs. The plane has served with the Navy for many years, but the last two squadrons were scheduled to be transferred to the Naval Reserve in 1992. A/F-18 Hornets will replace the A-7Es in the fleet. Fewer numbers of F-18s (85) are needed in an A/F-18-equipped carrier air wing than in a similar A-7E wing (94).

The A-7E made its combat debut in April 1970 when VA-146 and VA-147 were deployed on the USS America (CV-66). The A-7E was similar to the A-7B it replaced except for an improved weapons delivery system, the AVQ-7B head-up display, the ASN-91 tactical computer, the APQ-126 forward-looking radar, the ASN-90 inertial measurement set, and one 20-mm M61A1 gun instead of the two 20-mm MK-12 guns.

(U.S. Navy)

In this 1987 photo, three A-7E Corsairs of Attack Squadron 72 (VA-72) are flying in formation over a target range at Naval Air Station, Fallon.

This A-7E, assigned to China Lake for test purposes, was the first E version in the final lot to be produced.

With the E model, 535 were produced. The first flight test took place in November 1969. Many of these planes could very well still be on station with the Naval Reserve until past the turn of the century.

Other off-shoot designations abound for this interesting plane. There was a YA-7H designation that was a private venture (first flown in 1972). It incorporated a tandem two-seat configuration and was basically a training/combat version of the A-7E.

Also proposed by the manufacturer was a twin-engined development of the A-7E carrying the designation Vought A-529D. The proposal had the single TF41 engine replaced by two nonafterburning GE 404 powerplants, each producing 10,000 pounds of thrust. A fuselage length increase was required to accommodate the new propulsion system. Many of the components of the proposed aircraft would be compatible with the F-18. The concept was never continued.

Another designation was the little-known KA-7F. This proposed system was a carrier-based tanker to replace the KA-3B Skywarrior. It, too, ended early in the development stage. The A-7G, another never-produced model, was to be a version for the Swiss Air Force. The deal for production with that country was never struck, however, so the project died. The G model was to be based on the Air Force A-7D with an uprated TF41 powerplant and other equipment changes.

This 1988 shot shows two A-7Es, armed with AGM-65 Shrike missiles, from Attack Squadron 49 (VA-46) on the Aircraft Carrier America (CV-66).

This 1982 low-angle shot shows an A-7E assigned to Light Attack Squadron 46 (VA-46) on the Aircraft Carrier America (CV-66).

Two versions of the Corsair II were still serving with foreign air forces in the late 1980s. Because H was the next designation number in line, the A-7H nomenclature was given to the version for the Hellenic Air Force (Greece). Sixty planes were ordered for delivery between August 1975 and mid-1977. The first A-7H flew on its initial flight in May 1975. The TA-7H was the two-seat version of the aircraft of which five were ordered. Actually, the A-7H was a land-based version of the popular A-7E carrier version.

Unlike Greece, which received new production aircraft, Portugal bought a modernized version of existing aircraft. The Portuguese received 43 single-seat A-7Ps under a $250 million contract. Six two-seat TA-7Hs also were procured under the contract.

(LTV)

There are two countries besides the United States that are using the Corsair II. One is the Hellenic (Greek) Air Force, which ordered 60 A-7Hs that were basically a land-based version of the U.S. Navy's A-7E.

(LTV)

The A-7P designation was given to the version of the Corsair II procured by the Portuguese Air Force. Six two-seat TQ-7Hs would also be purchased.

This 1988 photo shows four A-7E Corsairs from the Attack Squadron 46 with arresting hooks deployed for landing.

An aerial starboard view of the USS Nimitz (CVN-68) underway with two A-7Es from Light Attack Squadron 82 (VA-82) in flight above.

Table 3-1. **Production List of All Versions of the U.S. Navy's A-7s.**

152580 ··· 152582	YA-7A		
152647 ··· 152685	A-7A		
153134 ··· 153273	A-7A		
154344 ··· 154360	A-7A		
154913 ··· 154929	A-7A	Deliveries Canceled	
154361 ··· 154573	A-7B	Deliveries of 154557—154573 Canceled	
156178 ··· 156417	A-7B	Deliveries Canceled	
156734 ··· 156800	A-7C		
156801 ··· 156890	A-7E		
157435 ··· 157648	A-7E	Deliveries of 157595—157648 Canceled	
158002 ··· 158028	A-7E		
158652 ··· 158681	A-7E		
158819 ··· 158842	A-7E		
159261 ··· 159308	A-7E		
159638 ··· 159661	A-7E		
159668 ··· 159679	A-7E		
159967 ··· 160006	A-7E		
160537 ··· 160566	A-7E		
160613 ··· 160618	A-7E		
160710 ··· 160739	A-7E		
160857 ··· 160886	A-7E	Deliveries of 160881—160886 Canceled	
159622 ··· 159667	A-7H		
159913 ··· 159966	A-7H		
161218 ··· 161222	TA-7H		U.S. Navy

Finally, there was also under consideration a company-proposed project coined the Corsair III. The concept was based on an A-7B airframe with a 27,600-pound thrust General Electric F110 afterburning engine. Minor structural changes—two structural plugs—would have been required. The fuel system would have had an update to accommodate the afterburning operation of the engine. Several high-tech changes were proposed to the ECM, avionics, and maneuvering systems. But alas, the system would never be built. Had it been, it certainly would have been the hottest of the Corsairs. It bears a marked similarity to the YA-7F program that would follow in the late 1980s.

=4=

Air Force A-7s

THERE'S such a thing as service pride. The Navy and the Air Force in this era quite simply like to develop their own aircraft without involvement from the other. But as aviation history has shown, it doesn't always work out that way.

Earlier than the A-7, the Air Force was ordered to adapt the Navy F-4 Phantom, a move that certainly worked out well for the Air Force. It happened again with the Corsair II, and again the jury came back with a positive decision.

Granted, the Air Force adopted the Navy Corsair II as one of its own, but the U.S. Air Force would derive a somewhat new model—the A-7D—in the process. The Air Force had been interested in the plane from early in its development. It had seen mission capabilities in the plane that were compatible to its own. The plane was viewed as an excellent platform for close air support of ground forces. In fact, the Air Force had earlier sent a small team from Edwards Air Force Base to evaluate the A-7A.

In 1968, Air Force Chief of Staff John McConnell and Senator Stuart Symington discussed the possible joint-service use of the aircraft. What eventually resulted that year was a decision for the Air Force to go with the Corsair II. But the Air Force made it very clear that there would be a number of significant changes required to satisfy the Air Force brass.

A-7D Modifications

The Air Force A-7D would, in the end, incorporate some 26 major modifications. These modifications would be agreed upon in April 1968, although some early testing using modified A-7As had actually started the month before.

This A-7D performed in an Aeronautical Systems Division (ASD) test at Wright-Patterson Air Force Base. The name of the test was AGILE, which stood for Air-craft Ground Induced Loads Excitation. The purpose of the testing was to determine how a fully loaded Corsair II would react to a battle-damaged runway. The AGILE equipment consisted of three independent hydraulic shakers that duplicated the input to the tires and landing gears on the plane during operation on the damaged runway surface.

Major differences in the A-7D included its more powerful engine, an improved avionics package that integrated the bombing and navigation systems with a computer and a flight information pictorial display, better survivability through better electronic countermeasures, more protective armor, the addition of fire-suppressing foam in the fuel tanks, and back-up control systems. Other changes included an awesome Gatling gun up front, an air refueling receptacle replacing a probe, a self-starter, improved brakes and landing gear, more precise delivery of ordnance capabilities, a damage assessment camera, major changes in the cockpit design, and a projected display of maps using color film.

Quite surprising was the fact that some of the Navy's shipboard features were retained. Strictly-carrier adaptions, such as the arrestor hook, were kept because of possible use with runway arresting devices in emergency landings and aborted takeoffs. Also retained was the folding wing design for combat revetment use and storage, and the space-saving notched rudder. Initially, the Air Force had thought about adding an afterburner to the existing powerplant, but the adoption of the new Rolls Royce TF41-A-1 easily provided the desired extra performance the Air Force felt it needed in its new plane. Allison Corporation would build the engine.

A little freeze job. That's what this A-7D is receiving in a cold test at the huge climatic chamber at Eglin Air Force Base, Florida. The Corsair II is dwarfed by a huge C-5A transport. This testing is a part of all Air Force aircraft full-scale development phases.

The A-7D that evolved ended up having the capability to carry a wide range of conventional ordnance, grossing out at more than 15,000 pounds on the six underway pylons and two fuselage-mounted weapon stations. The weapons include both air-to-air and air-to-surface missiles, general-purpose bombs rockets, and gun pods. The proven Gatlin M61A1 Vulcan 20-mm cannon, mounted in the port side of the fuselage, can be fired at rates up to 6,000 rounds per minute.

The aircraft possesses high-speed, low-altitude maneuverability under various weapon loads. It can loiter close to the target for up to two hours and is capable of extended range through in-flight refueling or external fuel tanks. The A-7D has an internal fuel capacity of 1,425 gallons and can add an additional 1,200 gallons in its external tanks. The first 26 A-7Ds were constructed with a probe-and-drogue refueling system, with all subsequent D models produced with a boom receptacle.

Robert McNamara, former Secretary of Defense, was so impressed with the improvements to the A-7D, especially in the avionics system, that he reduced the A-7D force structure from 24 to 23 fighter attack wings. The wings would be equipped with a mix of F-4s, F-111s, and A-7Ds. The increase in bombing accuracy expected from the new avionics system, he stated, "was such that one wing of the planned A-7D force could be eliminated and still achieve an overall increase in the target destructive capability of the A-7 force." Great things were being expected of the Corsair II.

The first two A-7Ds were accepted by the Air Force carrying the Navy TF-30 powerplant. Flight test activity was accomplished with this configuration until the new Allison engine was available. The planes were used in early testing of the aircraft at the LTV Aerospace facility in Dallas, Texas. The first flight of A-7D aircraft number three, equipped with the TF-41, was made on 26 September 1968 at Edwards Air Force Base. In December of that same year, the Air Force accepted the first A-7D completely fitted in accordance with the configuration requirements.

In a 1975 test flight, this A-7D was equipped with a digital flight control system. This was the first flight for the system.

In March of 1970, the capabilities of the A-7D were demonstrated in dramatic fashion. Two Air Force Corsair IIs were flown on a 3,502-mile unrefueled flight from Edwards Air Force Base, California, to Homestead Air Force Base, Florida, to show the deployment capability of the aircraft. Brigadier General Alton Slay, Commander of Edwards AFB, led the flight with Lt. Col. William Twinting, A-7D test director, at the controls of the second aircraft.

Deliveries of the A-7D started slowly in 1968 with five. These were followed by 12 in 1969, 57 in 1970, 128 in 1971, 88 in 1972, and 97 in 1973.

Production of 459 A-7Ds was completed in December 1976. But the Air Force also acquired another version of the bird, coined the A-7K. It was basically the same aircraft modified for training purposes with a second seat. Of the two-seat version, 31 were purchased.

One huge advantage the Air Force acquired with the D model was that it didn't have to duplicate the Navy's experience with the A model. An advantage to the Navy lay in the possibility of adapting the D model to Navy needs and creating a new Navy A-7. That's exactly what happened, leading the Navy to develop the E model, which was identical to the Air Force's A-7 except for a slightly different powerplant, an air turbine self-starter in place of the gas turbine starter, and minor changes in the radio navigation aids.

Minus its wings, this brand-new A-7D is unloaded from a Super Guppy transport aircraft at Edwards Air Force Base, California.

Delivery of the A-7Ds to the Tactical Air Command (TAC) began in September 1969. These were preproduction models used by a detachment of the 4525th Fighter Weapons Wing at Luke Air Force Base, Arizona. Later, the 312th Tactical Fighter Squadron conducted combat crew training. The first TAC operational wing to be equipped with the A-7D was the 354th Tactical Fighter Wing at Myrtle Beach Air Force Base, South Carolina. This wing started receiving its production model A-7Ds in September 1970. The wing would also be the first to see combat in Vietnam. Production of the complete run of A-7Ds was accomplished in December 1976.

The A-7D was one of the few new aircraft to be sent directly to Air National Guard units. With the A-7D, that process started in 1973. And even though the active Air Force no longer has any of the A-7Ds with operational units, there are a number of the D models still around at bases performing support missions.

One of the most highly publicized missions that A-7Ds are currently performing is with the 4450th Tactical Group at Nellis Air Force Base. At this location, 18 A-7Ds act as companion trainers for the F-117A stealth fighters, which are also assigned to the group. Although the A-7s don't get any of the publicity, they still perform a valuable contribution for the proving of the F-117A fighter.

Air Force A-7D Milestones

2 December 1965	The Secretary of Defense authorized the Air Force to develop and procure a D model of the Navy's A-7A aircraft. The aircraft would be used to support the Air Force tactical mission of close support.

(U.S. Air Force)

This right-side view of an A-7D is shown with a new camouflage paint scheme for use over desert and forest backgrounds. The test was performed in 1981.

(U.S. Air Force)

An A-7D of the 76th Tactical Fighter Squadron, 23rd Tactical Fighter Wing, air-dropping Mark-82 high-drag bombs at Tyndall Air Force Base, Florida.

6 January 1966	The Air Force A-7D Project Office was established with the initial cadre of Air Force personnel headed by Col. Robert Hails.
18–19 February 1966	An Air Force team initially evaluated the Navy A-7A fighter at the LTV facilities at Dallas. Major changes to the aircraft were recommended by the team in order to suit the aircraft to Air Force requirements.
8 August 1966	The Secretary of Defense approved the TF41 turbofan as the primary powerplant for the Air Force A-7D. This was a Rolls Royce engine of the Spey design that was licensed for production at the Allison Division of the General Motors Corp. in Indianapolis.
29 November 1966	A joint Navy/Air Force A-7 Program Office was established providing for a Navy Project Manager who functioned as the single central executive with the responsibility for overseeing all of the A-7 program.
January 1967	Approval of avionics system improvements was accomplished and consisted of the following components: tactical computer set, inertial measurement set, pilot head display set, doppler radar set, air data computer system, forward-looking radar system, armament station control unit and the projected map display system.
October 1967	Four U.S. Air Force pilots conducted a 14-flight evaluation of two instrumented A-7A aircraft at LTV.
24 October 1967	The first successful operation of the TF41 turbofan engine was conducted at the Rolls Royce plant in England.
December 1967	The Air Force Chief of Staff authorized a full go-ahead for the A-7D program.
22 January 1968	Secretary of Defense McNamara singled out the improvements in the avionics system planned for the A-7D as a major factor in the decision to reduce the force structure from 24 to 23 fighter attack wings.

April 1969	The first two A-7Ds were accepted by the Air Force. They were fitted with the Navy TF30-P-8 engines pending delivery of the first TF41-A-1 engines later in the year.
6 April 1969	The A-7D aircraft was flown for the first time.
30 June 1968	Funding for the A-7D procurement program for fiscal year 1967 and prior years was projected as $124.3 million for 12 aircraft. A total of $1.255 billion was projected for the procurement of 517 aircraft.
November 1968	The first flight of a TF41 engine powered A-7D with an Air Force pilot at the controls.
December 1968	The 150-hour endurance portion of the Military Qualification Test of the TF41-A-1 engine was completed.
30 June 1969	A-7D Aircraft number eight was delivered to Eglin Air Force Base, Florida, for Category II environmental tests in the climatic hangar.
20 August 1969	Start of formal A-7D Category II flight testing at Edwards Air Force Base.
December 1969	A three-wing force of A-7Ds was authorized, calling for procurement of a total of 387 aircraft.
June 1970	The A-7D/Maverick Missile flight test program was started at Holloman Air Force Base, New Mexico.
30 June 1970	The first phase of A-7D Category III testing was completed by the 4525th Fighter Weapons Wing at Luke Air Force Base.
September 1970	First operational A-7D squadron fully equipped.
March 1971	A-7D Initial Operational Capability (IOC) declared.

=5=

A-7s in the Air National Guard and Naval Reserve

DURING the late 1970s and 1980s, the A-7 was an aircraft in transition. It was fading away from the active forces and moving into the Air National Guard and Naval Reserve.

Deliveries of A-7Ds from active Air Force units started being transferred to the Air National Guard in 1973, with the Air National Guard having most of the Corsair IIs by the early 1980s. In fact, transfer of the A-7Ds to the Air National Guard actually started before the 459 A-7D production was completed in 1976. The Air National Guard got some brand-new A-7Ds directly from the manufacturer.

There was an additional version of the A-7 built specifically for the Air Force. The so-called A-7K was basically a two-seat version of the A-7D, with the first K version being converted from an existing A-7D. Although the A-7K was specifically designed as a trainer from the beginning, the model still retains full combat capabilities.

There were a number of minor changes on the A-7K. The refueling receptacle was relocated to the fuselage centerline, while the fuselage itself was lengthened some 34 inches. The big change in the aircraft, however, was the addition of the additional cockpit.

There were 31 A-7Ks constructed, with one going to each of the A-7 Air National Guard units. The remainder were assigned to the 152nd Tactical Fighter Group in Arizona.

(U.S. Air Force, Sgt. Joe Stahl)

A-7Ds of the 178th Tactical Fighter Group, the Ohio Air National Guard, are stationed at Springfield Municipal Airport.

These Air National Guard Corsair IIs haven't been just sitting there getting obsolete. There have been many improvements made to the trusty old birds to keep them up with the times.

Automatic maneuvering flaps were installed on all Air National Guard A-7Ds. The modification enabled the planes to accomplish a better turn radius and to increase the high angle of attack capabilities. The 127-mm flap is mounted on the existing wing flap's trailing edge.

(U.S. Air Force, Sgt. Joe Stahl)

This highly-effective weapon for the Corsair II is the GPU-51A 30-mm gun pod.

(U.S. Air Force)

One of the newest of the A-7 breed, this Arizona Air National Guard A-7K carries a 1979 tail number.

The pilot of this A-7D from the 127th Tactical Fighter Wing from Selfridge Air National Guard Base, Michigan, checks about getting a drink of jet fuel for his bird.

In 1982, a program was completed on 367 Air National Guard A-7Ds to modify them with the Pave Penny laser spot tracker pod. In the late 1980s, 80 A-7Ds and A-7Ks were upgraded with the so-called low-altitude night attack (LANA) modification. The first LANA-equipped aircraft (an A-7K) of the 152nd Tactical Fighter Squadron made its initial flight in October 1986. This system provided the Corsair II with basic daylight capabilities during nighttime operations. LTV also retrofitted 72 A-7Ds and 8 A-7Ks with forward-looking infrared (FLIR) and automatic terrain following (ATF) equipment to provide round-the-clock capability.

Also in the late 1980s, the Aeronautical Systems Division (ASD) at Wright-Patterson Air Force Base tested a new windshield for the A-7D fleet. The testing of the new piece of equipment was accomplished by the 162nd Tactical Fighter Group.

The windshield is assessed capable of withstanding strikes by birds weighing up to four pounds with speeds up to 550 miles per hour. The operational windshield could take strikes up to only about 178 miles per hour, so the improvement is quite obvious. The new windshield absorbs almost 10 times the impact energy of the original design, yet it weighs the same. The unit is constructed of multiple layers of polycarbonate material between two layers of acrylic.

The new windshield eliminated the cumbersome horseshoe-shaped frame that connected the three pieces of the original hardware. Production for 400 of the high-tech windshields was planned for mid-1989.

Built in 1973, this A-7K two-seater sits on the ramp at the Tucson International Airport. It's a member of the 162nd Tactical Fighter Group of the Air National Guard.

An A-7K from the 132nd Tactical Fighter Wing of the Iowa Air National Guard gets the chocks pulled in preparation for take off.

The Air Force also upgraded its ALG-119 ECM pod for the F-4, A-10, and the Corsair II. Finally, the improved 2,000-pound bomb (the I-2000) was qualified for use on the A-7.

Earlier, in 1976, an A-7D was involved with an interesting experiment testing a wing constructed almost entirely of reinforced graphite and boron fibers supported in an epoxy resin matrix. Later, eight other wings were tested on Air National Guard A-7Ds, but the advanced wing concept was never adopted.

In December 1988, a 13-inch wing crack was discovered in one of the Air National Guard A-7s. The crack caused the Air Force to inspect the entire A-7D and K fleet to determine if the cracks were typical in the whole fleet. The inspection was completed in late 1989 with approximately two-thirds of the planes requiring at least some repair. In November 1989, 357 of the total fleet of 365 aircraft were returned to operational duty.

LTV explained that most of the planes were repaired by teams from both the Air National Guard and LTV. There were eight A-7s that had to have the lower wing skin replaced. Engineers from the LTV contractor indicated that the cracks resulted from a more stressful use of the originally designed specifications when the plane was initially developed in the early 1960s.

When the crack was discovered, there was some concern whether the cracks would have any effect on the A-7 follow-on A-7F aircraft, which was in prototype production at the time (see chapter 7). LTV assured that the cracks would not affect that future program because the lower skin panels would be replaced on the new plane should that concept be adopted by the Air Force.

In 1989, 18 special duty A-7D/Ks, which had been assigned to the 4450th Tactical Group at Nellis AFB, Nevada, were transferred to the Air National Guard.

(U.S. Air Force)

An A-7D from the Virginia Air National Guard lines up in front of its name on the hangar at Richmond International Airport.

This A-7K gets a fill-up from this KC-135 of the Aeronautical Systems Division at Wright-Patterson Air Force Base.

Although the Corsairs of the Air National Guard have never seen the competition of combat with Guard pilots in the cockpits, the planes have participated with great success in another type of competition. It's called GUNSMOKE. The competition in 1987 featured two weeks of mock battle between 18 of top, active-duty Air Force Reserve and Air National Guard F-4, A-7, A-10, and F-16 units.

Quite simply, the every-other-year GUNSMOKE meets test the ability of the air crews to put their bombs on the target, to demonstrate pilot proficiency, and to determine ground crew effectiveness and pilot-crew cooperation.

Two A-7D Air National Guard Wings did well in the 1987 event. The 121st Tactical Fighter Wing from Rickenbacker Air National Guard Base, Ohio, finished fourth, while the 140th TFW from Buckley Air National Guard Base, Colorado, was sixth overall. The 121st's total of 8,862 points trailed the 388th Tactical Fighter Wing (with F-16As), winning a total of 9,165.5 points. The 121st was also the winner of the Maintenance Award at GUNSMOKE '83.

The 121st represented a typical A-7D Air National Guard unit. Two of the pilots were full-time Guardsman, while the three others were commercial pilots in their civilian careers.

Air National Guard A-7Ds have supported U.S. Air Force operations all over the world in recent years. One such effort was accomplished in the mid-1980s by the 138th Tactical Fighter Wing from Tulsa, Oklahoma. The unit's A-7Ds were the first-ever U.S. tactical aircraft in Grenada. The Corsair IIs supported a mock task force assault on the airport. Without doubt, the A-7s will be on guard with the Air National Guard until the beginning of the next century.

Two-place A-7Ks were provided directly to the Air National Guard. In this 1981 photo, testing is being performed on a new camouflage scheme.

Two A-7Ds from the Ohio National Guard line up for a fire power demonstration at the Dayton International Air Show in 1988.

A TAC A-7D comes in for a landing.

With its characteristic Flying Tiger shark's teeth showing, this A-7D from the 23rd Tactical Fighter Wing releases a pair of MR-82 high-drag bombs.

The official identification for this modified Corsair II would be YA-7F. Two prototypes were constructed using A-7Ds as starting points.

Each Air National Guard A7 unit has at least one of the two-seat A-7K versions. This A-7K is from the Arizona ANG.

This A-7D is assigned to Edwards Air Force Base as a special-mission aircraft. Following the assignment of A-7Ds to the Air National Guard, the only A-7s remaining in the active Air Force are aircraft like these.

A trio of A-7s show three of the many different color schemes the Corsair II has carried.

Corsair IIs assigned to the Air Force have had different paint schemes through the years. This flashy blue-and-gray coloring is one of the later ones used.

An A-7D basks in the sunset at Nellis AFB, Nevada, after a day of flying over the range during the Gunsmoke '87 competition.

SSgt. David Nolan

An Air Guard A07K two-seater pulls into position for a refueling from a KC-135 tanker. Note the position of the refueling receptacle behind the canopy. Also note that all six pylon positions are loaded: the inboard with fuel tanks and the outside pair on each side with bombs.

An A-7E comes in for the always-challenging aircraft carrier landing.

TOP LEFT AND BOTTOM: An A-7D prepares to taxi at the 140TFW, Buckley ANGB, Colorado, on its mission over the range during Gunsmoke '87 at Nellis AFB, Nevada.

TOP RIGHT: Bomb-load crew members from the Colorado ANGB, Buckley, Colorado, prepare bombs prior to loading them during the Gunsmoke '87 competition at Nellis AFB, Nevada, under the watchful eyes of the inspectors.

Liberal use of unit color schemes is allowed on the A-7s of the Air National Guard as is quite evident on the Little Sweetie 4 of the Ohio Air National Guard.

Since 1978, defense of the Panama Canal has been a mission of the Air National Guard. And that mission has always been performed by Corsair II units. During the late 1980s, several Air National Guard units deployed annually on rotations to Howard Air Force Base, Panama, taking their A-7 aircraft.

All Air National Guard A-7 units, including the one from Puerto Rico, share these responsibilities. The entire crew goes along on the deployment, which gives invaluable experience for aircraft maintenance under field conditions.

On the Navy side of the house, older active-duty A-7s were transitioned into Naval Reserve Units during the 1970s. The Naval reorganization of 1970 formed two Reserve Carrier Wings (CVWRs), and the A-7s would play heavily in filling those ranks. Initially, the aircraft to equip the new squadrons came from current stocks and included F-8H Crusaders, A-4L Skyhawks, and RF-8G Crusaders.

By the mid-1970s, however, even more modern aircraft were starting to make their appearance, including F-4 Phantoms and, of course, the A-7. The Point Mugu, Lemore, and Alameda Attack Squadrons traded in their tired A-4s for A-7As and, later, A-7Bs. The Corsairs were adorned with colorful Naval Reserve markings.

The A-7s of the Naval Reserve were faced with a serious problem in the early 1980s. The situation involved availability of engines for the A-7Bs. It was basically a problem of age because the Corsairs were getting old.

It was decided that something had to be done in order to keep the Naval Reserve up to fighting readiness. The decision was made to bring the A-7E into the Naval Reserves to allow transition of the F/A-18 Hornet into the active forces.

But don't get the idea that the A-7 is done with the Navy. The stubby little plane could well be around until the mid-1990s and probably even later with the Naval Reserves.

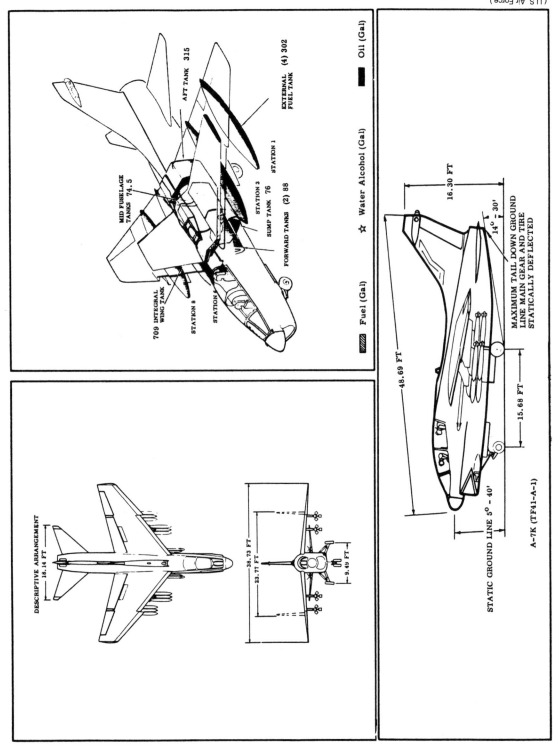

MID FUSELAGE TANKS 74.5

AFT TANK 315

STATION 3

SUMP TANK 76

STATION 1

FORWARD TANKS (2) 88

EXTERNAL FUEL TANK (4) 302

709 INTEGRAL WING TANK

STATION 8

STATION

Fuel (Gal)

☆ Water Alcohol (Gal)

Oil (Gal)

DESCRIPTIVE ARRANGEMENT

18.14 FT

38.73 FT

23.77 FT

9.49 FT

48.69 FT

16.30 FT

14° - 30'

MAXIMUM TAIL DOWN GROUND LINE MAIN GEAR AND TIRE STATICALLY DEFLECTED

15.68 FT

STATIC GROUND LINE 5° - 40'

A-7K (TF41-A-1)

Air National Guard A-7K details and characteristics.

52

EXTERNAL STORES

STATION LOADING

STORES	1	2	3	4	5	6	7	8	TOTAL
BOMBS									
M117A1 GP MC-1 Gas	3	1	2	-	-	2	1	3	12
or									
MK-20 Rockeye	1	4	2	-	-	2	4	1	14
MK-36 Destructor	4	6	2	-	-	2	6	4	24
MK-82 LDGP	6	-	4	-	-	4	-	6	20
MK-82 Snakeye	6	6	4	-	-	-	6	6	24
MK-83 LDGP	1	1	1	-	-	1	1	1	6
MK-84 LDGP	1	1	1	-	-	1	1	1	6
MK-84 EO-TV (GBU-8)	-	1	1	-	-	1	1	-	4
or									
MK-84 Laser (GBU-10), MK-82 Laser (GBU-12)	1	1	1	-	-	1	1	1	6
FIRE BOMBS									
BLU-27 Fire Bombs (Finned), BLU-1	1	3	1	-	-	1	3	1	10
BLU-27 Fire Bombs (unfinned)	1	1	1	-	-	1	1	1	6
BLU-52 Chemical Bombs	1	1	1	-	-	1	1	1	6
DISPENSER & BOMBS									
CBU-24	1	4	1	-	-	-	4	1	10
CBU-30/38	1	1	1	-	-	1	1	1	6
CBU-49/52/58	1	4	-	-	-	-	4	1	10
CBU-52/58/71	1	4	-	-	-	-	4	1	10
CBU-12, -46	2	-	-	-	-	-	-	2	4
ROCKET LAUNCHERS									
LAU-3/68	1	1	1	-	-	1	1	1	6
LAU-88/117	-	1	-	-	-	-	1	-	2
MISSILES									
AIM-9B, 9E, 9J	-	-	-	1	1	-	-	-	2
AGM-65A/B/D	-	3	-	-	-	-	3	-	6
FLARE DISPENSERS									
SUU-25C/A, 25E/A	-	1	-	-	-	-	1	-	2
SUU-42/A, 42A/A	1	-	-	-	-	-	-	1	2
GUN PODS									
SUU-23/A, GPU-5/A	-	-	1	-	-	1	-	-	2
ECM PODS									
AN/ALQ-71(V)-2-3	1	-	-	-	-	-	-	1	2
AN/ALQ-87									
AN/ALQ-101(V)-1-3-4-6									
AN/ALQ-119(V)-16-17									
AN/ALQ-131(V)									

A-7D/K external stores and station loading characteristics.

53

(John Farquhar)

Specialized ground support equipment aids these National Guard technicians in loading this bomb on an inboard A-7 pylon.

=6=

The A-7 in Combat

As a fighting machine, the A-7 has been endeared by almost every Navy and Air Force pilot that ever sat at its controls. It has done everything that was ever asked of it and, in many cases, much more.

One of the keys to that success was its flexibility. It was the first single-pilot aircraft ever designed that could deliver every special and conventional weapon in the inventory. During the Vietnam War, the Corsair II could deliver the 250-pound bomb, MK-81 Snakeye bombs, Walleye Glide bombs, Zuni rockets, Bullpup missiles, Shrike missiles, and 2,000-pound bombs. Name it and the A-7 could put it on the target.

The Corsair II saw combat in Southeast Asia with both the Navy and Air Force, with the Navy getting its A-7s there first in 1967. The first Navy Combat Air Wing (VA-147) had only five months of training with the then-new A-7A before steaming toward the combat zone. Surprisingly, during the training phase, the aircraft were still being delivered from the company to the USS Ranger. The last plane was delivered only two days before the aircraft carrier sailed. The wing was commissioned on 1 February 1967, graduation from the training phase occurring on 1 July 1967, and launch of the first combat strikes on 3 December 1967. For the first time in Navy aviation history, a new aircraft system was introduced into combat only two years after its first experimental test flight.

Many of the A-7A's characteristics were completely compatible with carrier combat operations. First, the configuration allowed the engine to be removed without breaking the fuselage or jacking the aircraft up to a required attitude. The

This A-7E takes off from the USS Independence (CV-62) as it was operating off the coast of Lebanon in support of the multinational peacekeeping forces in Beirut.

An A-7E is recovered on the deck of the USS American (VA-66) in the Gulf of Tomkin during the Vietnam War.

engine could also easily be slid out onto a dolly. This space-saving technique paid big dividends for carrier operations.

One of the real strong points of the A-7A and its follow-on versions was that it could take off weighing about 38,000 pounds of which 15,000 pounds could be external ordnance. That compared with the approximate 16,000 pounds of empty weight of the aircraft alone, the rest being fuel and cannon ammunition.

The additional armor plating under the pilot and engine and plating in front of the pilot paid big dividends from the survivability point of view. It was tough going on the low-level attacks, and any protection that could be provided was a big help. Reports were coming back of primitive, but very effective tactics, used by the Viet Cong, such as massing up to a thousand troops on the ground armed with rifles and light automatic weapons that were used to put up a vast cloud of hot lead in the path of the on-coming A-7s. After World War II, because of the emphasis on nuclear delivery capabilities, interest in aircraft armor had declined, but this experience brought it back in a big hurry.

Another of the desirable characteristics of the Navy A-7 in that giant conflict of the 1960s and 1970s was the aircraft's maintainability, allowing for fast turn-around aboard the carriers. Key features of the Corsair II that allowed this capability were the waist-high gun-loading characteristic and the complete absence of complicated ground support equipment. It was possible to accomplish 90 percent of all the maintenance on the Corsair at ground level.

Some 15 months later, the A-7B model also entered combat. In just over a year after that, the A-7E was the final version of the Corsair II to see the fire of battle.

In February of 1971, A-7Es staging off two carriers made a major effort at hitting enemy truck maneuvers. The A-7s accomplished computer release of flares over targeted road segments that was followed by visual delivery of seeds that allowed the enemy minimal chances of spotting the emplaced mine fields. The A-7 was involved in many large strike operations and performed in magnificent fashions with an excellent success rate until the end of the American involvement in the conflict.

The Air Force involvement with the A-7 in Vietnam is not nearly as well documented as that of the Navy, but the little bird was also there for land-based operations. The remarkable record of the 354th Tactical Fighter Wing got scant coverage in the press, but they were there making a very large contribution. The 354th's Corsairs arrived at Korat Royal Thai Air Force Base in mid-October of 1972, and its 72 A-7Ds flew some 4,000 sorties between October 16th and the end of December when American participation ended.

During its 10 weeks of combat, the wing dropped nearly 25,000 bombs, most of them of the Mark 82 500-pound variety. The accuracy was excellent with an average miss distance of about 10 meters.

The role of the Air Force's A-7Ds was to replace the prop-powered A-1 Skyraider, which flew its last mission in Southeast Asia in November 1972. Because the A-7s would be the aircraft working with the HH-53 choppers instead of the A-1s, it was necessary for the Corsair IIs to fly loitering patterns. This technique caused the Corsairs to burn more fuel and therefore require more refueling oper-

(U.S. Navy)

An A-7E from VA-146 is ready for launching off the flight deck of the USS Constitution (CVA-64) for a 1972 Vietnam air strike.

(U.S. Navy)

A-7Es taxi into position on the flight deck of the Carrier USS Kitty Hawk. The planes are loaded with MK20 rockets and antitank cluster bombs. The A-7E on the right is carrying a Shrike antiradar missile on its center pylon.

58

ations. During normal operations with the HH-53s, six Corsair IIs were assigned to each mission.

The A-7D was a huge improvement over the A-1 in terms of the increase in ordnance they could carry. Normally, in these search-and rescue missions, the Corsair IIs carried two CBU-38s along with pods of 2.75-inch rockets and WP rockets.

Two A-7Ds were lost during the stay in Thailand. One of the losses occurred as a result of a collision with a Forward Air Controller (FAC) aircraft over Laos. Another of the planes went down over North Vietnam. The first pilot was captured after he ejected, but he was released at the end of American involvement in 1973. The other pilot was never accounted for.

Many of the A-7D design characteristics were also found to be highly effective by Air Force pilots and crews. The D model proved to be very easy to maintain in a combat environment. It had a minimal abort rate of only about 0.3 percent and an air abort rate of 0.5.

The A-7D's electronic suite was also absolutely super, particularly the operation of the forward-looking radar, the doppler, inertial measuring system, and the radar altimeter. The data provided by these systems enabled accurate delivery of bombs and 20-mm shells on the target area. The systems were also used for accurate straight-and-level bombing, radar offset bombing, and other maneuvers.

Another big plus for the A-7D and for Seventh Air Force planners was the length of the plane's legs. The A-7Ds were able to operate, completely combat loaded, without refueling from essentially all of Southeast Asia. A typical mission was for a 350-nautical mile radius. That radius took in all of South Vietnam and most of North Vietnam. Carrying two 300-gallon wing tanks and eight Mark 82 bombs, along with a thousand rounds of 20-mm ammunition, the A-7D had about a half hour in the target area and 2,300 pounds of fuel reserve to return to Korat. By cutting that fuel margin down to about 1,500 pounds, the combat radius could be increased to an impressive 480 miles, still without refueling.

The A-7D's range also came in very handy with both night escort missions for the AC-130 gunships and also in search-and-rescue missions. The Corsair was so good for that former mission because the Corsairs could stay up with the gunships for an hour and a half. The A-7Ds often performed flak suppression functions when they were escorting the AC-130s, a task that wasn't described as very much fun by participating pilots.

The Corsair II was a heavy participator in the final Linebacker II operation with A-7s from both the Navy and Air Force doing their thing. For the Navy, it would end continuous A-7 operations since late 1967. In all, the A-7s from both the Navy and Air Force flew over 100 sorties supporting that final effort. In the whole Vietnam conflict, the number of total A-7 sorties amounted to over 100,000!

An interesting footnote to A-7 operations in Southeast Asia is the fact that birds from neither service ever got an enemy aircraft kill even though both carried the AIM-9 air-to-air missile. But antiaircraft combat was not what the stubby little bird was designed to accomplish. Carrying heavy ordnance loads and putting them accurately on the target was its strong point, and it did it well.

(U.S. Navy)

A-7Es along with numerous F-4s and A-6s clutter the deck of this aircraft carrier.

(U.S. Air Force)

An amazing photo of an Air Force A-7D getting a refueling from a KC-135 in the skies of Southeast Asia.

The Vietnam War was not the last time the A-7 has seen combat action. There have been several occasions since that the A-7 has been called upon for support. Navy A-7Es have also seen participation in additional confrontations, first in Lebanon and then later in Grenada. In the former activity, A-7Es from the USS Independence flew missions in the eastern Mediterranean. The A-7Es and accompanying A-6 Intruders, attacked by rebel positions, had to face heavy surface-to-air missile opposition. An A-7E from the USS Independence was lost, while a second Corsair from the same carrier was badly damaged but made it back to the ship.

In the close-to-home attack on Grenada, Navy A-7Es orbited in the immediate target area. They provided support to the ground troops when it was needed.

Then the well-publicized raid on Libya in 1986 had Navy A-7Es out again. In conjunction with 18 F-111s staged from England, 15 A-6E Intruders and A-7Es struck two Libyan bases near Benghazi. All of the Corsairs returned safely to their carriers, but one F-111 was lost in the raid.

The A-7 is truly a plane that has paid its dues in combat.

=7=

The Future

THE Corsair II has proved itself as an outstanding combat performer for both the Air Force and Navy during its illustrious history. Over those years there have been many considerations and deliberations for making the A-7 even better, but none of those proposals ever reached fruition.

But as the 1980s progressed, the costs of new aircraft have gone up and the defense budget has gone down. Consequently, a new proposal known variously as the A-7 PLUS, A-7 Strikefighter, and finally, the YA-7F was born and funded.

The plan involved modifying two Air Force A-7D fleet aircraft (one each from the New Mexico and Oklahoma Air National Guard) for ambitious new mission requirements. The airframe modification program was one of the most extensive upgrades ever attempted on an in-service aircraft.

The program began in June 1985 when the Air Force issued a Request for Information (RFI) for an interim solution to the Close Air Support/Battlefield Air Interdiction (CAS/BAI) requirement. Involved in the mission requirement was close air support on the front lines and air strikes deep within enemy territory. The new plane would play an important part in the way the U.S. Army intends to fight in the next war. The response from LTV was, not surprisingly, a modification of the Corsair II.

The close air-support mission would work directly with Army forces that are engaged with the enemy on the battlefield. The air interdiction aircraft would need the capability to challenge the enemy forces that are about to reach the front lines. As of late 1989, the forces to accomplish that important mission consisted

(LTV)

An early artist's concept of how the A-7 PLUS would look. It is easy to see that the increased fuselage length would give the plane a whole new look.

of nine fighter wings, six wings of A-10s, and three wings of Air National Guard A-7Ds. The concept is currently referred to in U.S. military doctrine as the "Air-Land Battle."

The modified A-7 was not the only one considered for this important role. In all, there would be five aircraft considered. The interesting point in this competition was that not a single one of the aircraft would be new planes; all would be modifications of existing aircraft.

The favorite of the competition, as of this 1990 writing time period, was an attack modification to the F-16 Fighting Falcon, a plane that was in mass production at the General Dynamics plant in Fort Worth, Texas. The modifications on the plane were to have included the Pave Penny laser spot tracker, a 30-mm gun, and significant survivability improvements. It was rated as the heavy favorite.

An upgraded A-10 aircraft was another plane considered in the competition. This relatively slow aircraft already had a number of qualities that would enable it to accomplish the CAS/BAI mission, including two-engine reliability and the powerful Gatling Gun installation in its nose. The McDonnell Douglas AV-8B, with its very desirable short takeoff and landing capabilities, was also given a look. Even the Navy A/F-18 Hornet was considered.

In times of great pressure, to reduce the large U.S. defense budget, as was the case as the 1980s came to an end, the technique was to examine every possible system to determine the best answer for accomplishing the mission in the

Operations during 1988 when build-up work was underway on the YA-7F advanced Corsair II prototypes. Here, the forward fuselage section of the former A-7D is moved in a sling.

most economical manner. That's why there was so much interest in pursuing the A-7F modification. LTV officials felt that an extremely effective aircraft could be produced at a considerably lower cost than some of the other alternatives. But it wasn't the smooth sailing that had been hoped for in the fabrication of the YF-7A prototypes.

Officials had hoped that the first prototype would be able to take to the air in April 1989, but that event didn't take place until November of that year. LTV officials indicated that the program had fallen behind because the program had gotten too ambitious. Instead of sticking to the modifications required to accommodate the new engine and electronic systems, the company had made additional modifications that were more sophisticated than necessary.

Finally, though, the first of the prototypes did fly on 29 November 1989. The flight took place from LTV Aircraft Products Group facility at Dallas. The flight began with an afterburner-enhanced takeoff, lasted one hour and ten minutes, and included functional checks of the aircraft's systems. The pilot for the flight was Jim Read, the LTV chief test pilot.

The flight was but the first of an extensive evaluation of a 10-month duration. The program would be conducted at the Air Force Flight Test Center at Edwards Air Force Base, California. During that time, the Air Force would evaluate the aircraft's enhanced performance and handling qualities obtained from the

(LTV)

A rear view of the front fuselage section that was extensively modified. The fuse-lage became part of the first A-7F.

improved thrust and aerodynamics. Needless to say, hopes were high for success of the program, but only time would tell whether this aircraft would become the standard for modifying the complete 335 A-7D fleet, or just become another experimental prototype sitting somewhere in a boneyard or aircraft museum.

The modifications included a new afterburning engine and a forward-looking infrared (FLIR) system along with substantial aerodynamic, performance, and structural improvements. The long-range plan for the company would be to eventually modify all the Air National Guard planes. The U.S. Navy, however, showed no interest in the modification of their A-7E aircraft, preferring instead to concentrate on the F-18 upgrade.

LTV estimated that the cost of this modification would be approximately half that of a new aircraft, but it would still have close to the same capabilities. The Air Force gave its approval to the LTV proposal, over the submissions of three other countries, and $35 million was appropriated in fiscal year 1987 toward full-scale development of the aircraft, which would be renamed A-7 Plus by the contractor. In May 1987, the Air Force Aeronautical Systems Division awarded LTV a contract to build the two prototype aircraft. In October 1987, the Air Force officially designated the two prototype aircraft as YA-7Fs.

With Jim Read, LTV's chief test pilot, at the controls, the first YA-7F conducted low- and high-speed taxi tests prior to the first flight on 29 November 1989.

(LTV)

Jim Read, LTV's chief test pilot, stands in front of the YA-7F. The saga of this plane reminded many of the transformation of the F-8 to the A-7 configuration.

(LTV)

LTV technicians reinstall the wing on the first of the YF-7A prototypes. The modernized A-7s will incorporate greatly increased capabilities over the original design.

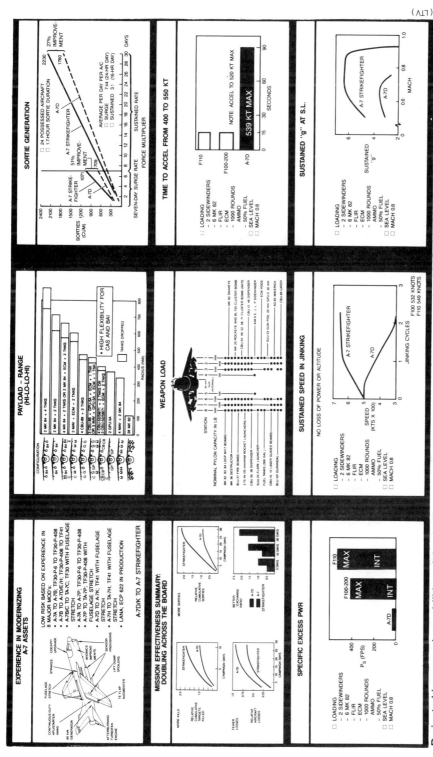

Projected increased capabilities of the A-7F.

Extensive wind tunnel testing was accomplished on YA-7F models at the U.S. Air Force Arnold Engineering Development Center (AEDC). Because the aircraft's basic structure was altered, tests had to prove that safe weapon separation could be accomplished. The intent of the testing was to ensure that the stores, when released from the aircraft, would not fly back into the plane, causing loss of aircraft and pilot.

Testing was accomplished in AEDC's 4-foot transonic wind tunnel using 1/20 scale models of the aircraft and stores. Store models included several bombs, missiles, and fuel tanks. An A-7D model from the AEDC inventory was modified into a YA-7F by engineers who designed and fabricated the necessary parts. AEDC's unique captive trajectory system was used by engineers to separate the stores from the aircraft at Mach numbers from .40 to .90 (approximate airspeeds of 325-to-675 miles per hour).

The modifications are significant to these two A-7Ds and address just about every part of the aircraft and its systems. Following is a discussion of the changes to the airframe, engine, electronics, ordnance capability, and future growth.

Airframe

Modifications to the A-7's fuselage and wings would allow the plane to operate out of austere airfields with runways as short as 3,000 feet. The fuselage upgrades will also enhance the plane's structural integrity and allow for improved electronic and fuel systems.

The fuselage will be stretched in two places: 29.5 inches forward and 18 inches aft. This length increase provides for proper aircraft balance and also provides space for additional avionics and fuel.

There are also considerable upgrades on the wings with an LTV-developed trailing edge flap augmenter high-lift device, lift dump spoilers, and strakes. The augmented flaps permit slower landing speeds, while the spoilers work automatically when the aircraft touches down, decreasing the landing roll. The strakes help keep the aircraft stable when maneuvering at high angles of attack. They also increase the maximum lift generated by the wing, resulting in about a 10 percent increase in turn rate for the YA-7F. The new plane also has a new vertical tail fin cap for additional stability during high angle-of-attack flight.

Engine

The aft section of the aircraft is modified to accept the Pratt & Whitney F100-PW-220 engine and is fitted with a new engine removal door and tail cone, although the GE110 engine is also compatible with the airframe. The performance is significantly greater than the original engine, with nearly twice as much thrust that provides about five times greater acceleration. Speeds of Mach 1.0 and above is possible with this aircraft as well as the capability to accelerate from 400 to 550 knots in about 15 seconds.

Also, dramatically improved thrust should enable the YA-7F to sustain about seven "Gs," which means that during high-speed maneuvers the aircraft should sustain gravity forces much more effectively than the original A-7 design. The

Workers at LTV install the new F-100 powerplant in the first YA-7F prototypes. The stretched aircraft with its new afterburning engine completed test operations in 1989. The increased thrust of the new aircraft could provide the plane with improved capability for air-to-ground missions and enhanced survivability well into the 1990s and beyond.

new engine should provide the plane with greater agility and decreased exposure time in the target area, thus making it more difficult to track, find, and hit.

The increased performance capability of the new powerplant will enable the new plane to have a speed in excess of 650 knots. That impressive capability can be demonstrated with a full combat load and 50 percent fuel loading. The A-7F will also have the capability of pulling 6G turns up to speeds of Mach .9. The A-7F will weigh considerably different depending on the type of powerplant it's carrying. When the plane is equipped with the Pratt & Whitney F100 engine, the plane will weigh about 800 pounds less than its GE counterpart. The A-7F will weigh almost 23,000 pounds with the P&W powerplant and about 23,900 pounds with the GE F110.

Electronic Upgrades

The YA-7F includes the low-altitude night attack (LANA) system, permitting low-altitude navigation and target detection, day or night or under the weather. To configure the A-7D with LANA required integration of advanced cockpit, radar, and system improvements for dramatically improved mission effectiveness and required pilot workload. One of the main components of

(LTV)

The first YA-7F rolls out of the LTV Dallas facility. The plane would perform its first flight test late in 1989, with the decision on whether the plane will be produced still in doubt in the early 1990s.

(LTV)

The YA-7F is shown conducting taxi tests prior to its first flight on 29 November 1989. The aft section of the plane was modified with a new engine removal door and tail cone.

LANA is the FLIR radar system which is integrated with the A-7's AN/APQ-126 radar and the automatic flight control system (AFCS) to all for automatic terrain following. This capability lets the pilot concentrate closely on his attack mission by allowing him to fly low-level into a target area while avoiding hazardous terrain.

Ordnance Capability

The YA-7F is able to carry flexible payloads of up to 17,380 pounds of virtually any munition available in the current U.S. Air Force inventory on the aircraft's six wing and two fuselage-mounted pylons. The fuselage-mounted 20-mm gun is retained along with the thousand-round ammunition capacity and the two AIM-9 Sidewinder air-to-air missiles. Other ordnance possibilities include the Mark 82 Snakeye, Mark 20 Rockeye, and BL-755 cluster bomb, and AGM-65 Maverick air-to-ground missile (HVM), which is an air-launched antitank missile that uses kinetic energy to destroy armored vehicles.

Future Capability

The YA-7F will be configured to handle future growth potential should it ever be necessary. As modified, the plane could later be equipped with a new inertial measurement navigation system, and antijamming communications suite, and other command, control, communications, and intelligence systems essential to CAS/BAI including the low-altitude navigation and targeting infrared night system (LANTIRN).

(LTV)

With its afterburner on, the YA-7F prototype takes to the air for the first time.

Looking at the YA-7F makes you realize that the Corsair II has taken on a completely new look. It has a more graceful image. The plane doesn't seem to have that stubby look it had for so long. Looks more like an F-8 Crusader again! And with its significant modifications, it's going to be one heck of a more capable fighting machine.

The YA-7F will have greatly increased survivability, greater maneuverability, higher performance, reduced takeoff roll, greater payload capability, and much improved electronic capabilities. It's going to be a great airplane.

There are critics who insist that use of a new airplane instead of the proposed upgrade of an old airplane is a more cost-worthy investment. But whatever the result of this upgrade, the YA-7F, which might eventually be called the A-7F, will be the last of the Corsair IIs. The plane was born in the 1960s with a Navy supersonic mission, later transformed to a subsonic bomb carrier, and finally has become a close air support fighter of the 1990s.

Index

Other Bestsellers of Related Interest

THE B-1 BOMBER: Aero Series, Vol. 35—2nd Edition—William G. Holder

From its earliest beginnings in 1955 to production of the final B-1B in 1988 to predictions for its future, this lavishly illustrated volume gives you the entire picture. Covered in this comprehensive volume are the history, design details, industrial problems, technological breakthroughs, and challenges of the B-1B. Also discussed are recent avionics improvements, including enhanced forward-looking terrain-following radar, which give the B-1B unparalleled navigation and weapons delivery accuracy. 128 pages, 109 illustrations. Book No. 20616, $10.95 paperback only

BEECHCRAFT STAGGERWING—Peter Berry

Featuring never-before-published facts and photographs from the archives of the Beechcraft Staggerwing Museum Foundation, this book is a complete illustrated record of the colorful history of one of the classic aircraft of the 1930s. Beginning with the early experiences of the Staggerwing's designer, aviation pioneer Walter F. Beech, Berry describes the Staggerwing's development and production, its foreign and domestic uses, and its record-breaking races. This is truly a necessary addition to the library of any classic aircraft buff. 160 pages, 104 illustrations, 8 full-color pages. Book No. 3410, $14.95 paperback only

BOEING 737: Aero Series, Vol. 37—David H. Minton

This book offers an accurate and complete historical record of the Boeing 737, including commercial uses, prototypes, variations, and military applications. More than 100 line drawings and photographs illustrate the 737 from every possible angle, showing details on wings, tails, engines, pylons, cockpit interiors, galleys, instruments, cabin layouts, and liveries in close-up detail. Includes a detailed scale modeler's section and eight pages of full-color photographs. 88 pages, 8-page full-color insert. Book No. 20618, $10.95 paperback only

THE McDONNELL DOUGLAS F-4 PHANTOM: Aero Series, Vol. 36—Robert F. Dorr

The F-4 Phantom was the biggest, fastest, most expensive and—some say—ugliest fighter of its time. It was the standard against which every other jet fighter was measured. Dorr has assembled the whole story of the F-4, complete with dozens of detailed photographs of actual jets and many personal interviews with Phantom pilots. This definitive work on the design, development, and combat use of the famous McDonnell F-4 Phantom traces three decades. 96 pages, 8-page full-color insert. Book No. 20617, $10.95 paperback only

BOEING B-52 STRATOFORTRESS: Aero Series, Vol. 34—2nd Edition—William G. Holder and Robert Woodside

For more than three decades the B-52 global bomber has constituted the vital third leg of America's nuclear deterrent triad. The latest airframe modifications, engines, electronic systems, and ordnance carried, including the air-launched cruise missile, are discussed and illustrated here. 96 pages, 89 illustrations, 8 color pages. Book No. 20615, $10.95 paperback only

McDONNELL DOUGLAS F-15 "EAGLE": Aero Series, Vol. 28—James Perry Stevenson

This aircraft was most recently voted to be sold to Saudi Arabia. Here, history of "Eagle" versions and applications are recorded. Facts about its design, performance, and missions are complemented throughout by drawings and photographs. With a string of "firsts" to its credit, the F-15 makes fascinating reading! 103 pages, Fully illustrated. Book No. 20604, $10.95 paperback only

THE McDONNELL DOUGLAS OH-6A HELICOPTER: Aero Series, Vol. 38—Donald J. Porter

Developed in the early 1960s and still in service today, the OH-6A helicopter earned a reputation in the Vietnam War as a dependable, high-performance machine. Widely used as both airborne ambulance and observation craft, the OH-6A was uniquely suited to its roles. Porter examines the OH-6A's birth, development, physical characteristics, current status, and combat roles. 96 pages, 8-page full-color insert. Book No. 20619, $10.95 paperback only

AMERICAN AVIATION: An Illustrated History—Joe Christy, with contributions by Alexander T. Wells, Ed.D.

Here, in a comprehensive, well-researched sourcebook, Christy and Wells have taken the history of American aviation and transformed it into a fascinating story of people, machines, and accomplishments that is as entertaining as it is informative. With its hundreds of excellent photographs, this is a book that every aviation enthusiast will want to read and reread! 400 pages, 486 illustrations. Book No. 2497, $25.95 paperback only

THE LUFTWAFFE: A Photographic Record 1919-1945—Karl Ries
Written by Germany's premier Luftwaffe historian!

This book is a behind-the-scenes look at the Luftwaffe from a noted author who has studied and written about the subject for more than 20 years. Author Karl Ries provides an actual account of the German Air Force. Hundreds of previously unpublished photographs and accompanying text chronologically tell the Luftwaffe's origins, rise, combat, and ultimate decline. 240 pages, 450 illustrations. Book No. 22384, $24.95 hardcover only

GENERAL DYNAMICS F-111 *"AARDVARK"*: Aero Series, Vol. 29—Jay Miller

General Dynamics' awesome variable-sweep-wing F-111 is unquestionably the most controversial operational warplane of our time—politically sensitive, economically catastrophic, and mechanically overwhelming. This book provides a synopsis of its construction and a review of its service career. 104 pages, illustrated. Book No. 20606, $9.95 paperback only

THE BLOND KNIGHT OF GERMANY—Raymond F. Toliver and Trevor J. Constable

The fascinating biography of the most successful fighter ace in the history of aerial warfare—Erich Hartmann whose 352 victories amounted to more than six times those of the top U.S. ace! You'll relive Hartmann's extraordinary aerial achievements, the ordeals suffered during 10 years of post-war imprisonment by the Soviet Union, and his role in the new West German Air Force. 352 pages, 168 illustrations. Book No. 24189, $16.95 paperback only

IF YOU ENJOY TAB'S AERO SERIES BOOKS, YOU'LL LOVE DETAIL & SCALE AND COLORS & MARKINGS:

PROFUSELY ILLUSTRATED GUIDES FOR MILITARY AND AVIATION HISTORIANS AND MODELING ENTHUSIASTS

THE DETAIL & SCALE SERIES:

Each *Detail & Scale* volume includes technical data and tables, performance data, mission profiles, historical and developmental summaries, ordnance and armament coverage, and a scale modeler's section with kit reviews and decal listings. The books are 72 pages in length, with eight pages in full color, and more than 200 illustrations. Bound in an oversized 8-1/2″ × 11″ format, volumes in *Detail & Scale* cost just $9.95.

Vol. 2, B-17 Flying
 Fortress, Part 1
 (Production Versions)
Vol. 3, F-16 A & B
 Fighting Falcon
Vol. 4, F-111 Aardvark
Vol. 6, F-18 Hornet
 (Developmental &
 Early Production
 Aircraft, Part 1)
Vol. 7, F-4 Phantom II,
 Part 2 (USAF F-4E &
 F-4G)
Vol. 8, F-105
 Thunderchief
Vol. 9, F-14A Tomcat
 (SU-22 Killer)

Vol. 10, B-29
 Superfortress, Part 1
Vol. 11, B-17 Flying
 Fortress, Part 2
Vol. 12, F-4 Phantom II,
 Part 3 (USN & USMC)
Vol. 13, F-106 Delta Dart
 (Ultimate Interceptor)
Vol. 14, F-15 Eagle—2nd
 Edition
Vol. 15, F9F Panther (1st
 Navy Jet to See
 Combat)
Vol. 16, F9F Cougar
 (Grumman's 1st
 Swept-Wing Fighter)

Vol. 17, F11F Tiger
 (Navy's First
 Supersonic Fighter)
Vol. 18, B-47 Stratojet
Vol. 19, A-10 Warthog
 (The Tank Killer)
Vol. 20, B-17 Flying
 Fortress, Part 3
Vol. 21, F-101 Voodoo
Vol. 22, A-7 Corsair II
Vol. 23, Boeing 707 and
 AWACS
Vol. 24, The A-6 Intruder,
 Part 1 (Bomber and
 Tanker Versions)

Vol. 25, The B-29
 Superfortress, Part 2
 (Derivatives)
Vol. 26, F6F Hellcat
Vol. 27, B-52
 Stratofortress
Vol. 28, AV-8 Harrier,
 Part 1 (USMC
 Versions)
Vol. 29, USS Lexington
Vol. 30, F4F Wildcat
Vol. 31, F-8 Crusader
Vol. 32, A-4 Skyhawk
 (Navy and Marine)
Vol. 33, F-100 Super Sabre
Vol. 34, USS America
Vol. 35, F-102 Delta Dagger

THE COLORS & MARKINGS SERIES:

The *Colors & Markings Series* was designed to provide an affordable source for detailed information on the paint schemes, squadron markings, special insignia, and nose art carried by many of the most important aircraft in aviation history. Each volume feature outstanding photos—at least 50 in color and more than 200 in black and white, spread throughout the book. *Colors & Markings* volumes are 64 pages long, in an 8-1/2″ × 11″ format, and cost only $11.95. Special expanded 80-page editions (such as Vols. 6, 10, and 12) treat high-interest subjects with even more color photographs, at a cost of $14.95.

Vol. 1, F-106 Delta Dart
Vol. 2, F-14 Tomcat, Part
 1 (Atlantic Coast
 Markings)
Vol. 3, F-4C Phantom II,
 Part 1
Vol. 5, A-6 Intruder

Vol. 6, U.S. Navy
 Adversary Aircraft
Vol. 7, Special Purpose,
 C-130 Hercules
Vol. 8, F-14 Tomcat, Part
 2 (Pacific Coast
 Markings)

Vol. 9, A-7E Corsair II
 (U.S. Navy Atlantic
 Coast Post-Vietnam
 Markings)
Vol. 10, U.S. Navy and
 USMC CAG Aircraft,
 Part 1 (Fighters)

Vol. 11, U.S. Air Force
 Aggressor
 Squadrons
Vol. 12,
 MiG Kill Markings
 from the Vietnam War
Vol. 13, F-4E Phantom II